Monster Science

GHOSTS
AND ATOMS

BY JODI WHEELER-TOPPEN, PHD • ILLUSTRATED BY ESTUDIO HAUS

Consultant:
Roman Boulatov, PhD
Assistant Professor
Department of Chemistry
University of Illinois

CAPSTONE PRESS
a capstone imprint

Graphic Library is published by Capstone Press,
151 Good Counsel Drive, P.O. Box 669, Mankato, Minnesota 56002.
www.capstonepub.com

Books published by Capstone Press are manufactured with paper
containing at least 10 percent post-consumer waste.

Library of Congress Cataloging-in-Publication Data
Wheeler-Toppen, Jodi.
 Ghosts and atoms / by Jodi Wheeler-Toppen.
  p. cm.—(Graphic library. Monster science)
 Includes bibliographical references and index.
 Summary: "In cartoon format, uses ghosts to explain the science of atoms"—Provided
by publisher.
 ISBN 978-1-4296-6581-0 (library binding)
 ISBN 978-1-4296-7329-7 (paperback)
 1. Atoms—Juvenile literature. 2. Ghosts—Juvenile literature. 3. Graphic novels. I. Title.
QC173.16.W545 2012
 539.7—dc22   2011004487

Editor
Anthony Wacholtz

Art Director
Nathan Gassman

Designer
Ashlee Suker

Production Specialist
Eric Manske

Printed in the United States of America in Stevens Point, Wisconsin.
032011   006111WZF11

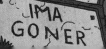

TABLE OF CONTENTS

CHAPTER 1

THE TINY WORLD OF ATOMS

An old house looms on a hill on a dark and stormy night.

Inside the house ...

... a black cat leaps from a table after being burned by a candle's wax.

The black cat, table, candle, and wax all have something in common. They are made of matter.

Everything in the world is made of matter, but matter is made of something too. All matter is made up of tiny particles called atoms.

AM I MADE OF ATOMS TOO?

particle—a very small piece or amount of something

Imagine a brick wall that is made of individual bricks. Like the bricks, atoms are the pieces that make up matter.

ZZZZZ

Atoms are tiny. If you chopped a candle into tiny pieces and put them under a microscope, you still wouldn't see any atoms.

For most of history, scientists have been learning about atoms without having any way to look at them.

The makeup of matter has puzzled scientists for centuries. In ancient Greece, Aristotle claimed that everything was made out of combinations of four things: air, water, fire, and earth.

For more than 2,000 years, Aristotle's view of matter was accepted by most people.

In the 1600s Robert Boyle thought that there were more elements than just air, water, fire, and earth. He experimented to find out what made up substances.

He tried to break down chemicals and turn them into simpler chemicals. If he couldn't break the chemical down, he said it was an element.

element—a substance that can't be broken down into a simpler substance

In 1771 Joseph Priestley showed that Aristotle's ideas were wrong. He found that air contained more than one type of gas. It wasn't an element after all!

HEY, I'M NOT AN ELEMENT EITHER!

For the next 200 years, scientists tried to identify new elements. They mixed and burned chemicals. They bubbled gases through any liquid they could think of. They even jolted things with electricity.

But the question remained: What made up the elements? In 1808 John Dalton said that elements are made of billions of tiny pieces that are all alike. He called the pieces "atoms." Each element had its own type of atom.

But discovering atoms wasn't enough for scientists. They wanted to know what atoms were made of.

In the late 1800s John Thompson found a particle smaller than an atom that he called an "electron." He said that atoms were like a bowl of pudding full of raisins. Most of an atom was like a smooth pudding, but there were electrons sprinkled in it like raisins.

In 1911 Ernest Rutherford did an experiment to find out what was inside atoms. He discovered that atoms have a lot of empty space. But he also found something thick and heavy in the center. He later called it the nucleus.

MAYBE YOU'RE AN ATOM. YOU'RE A LOT OF EMPTY SPACE WITH A HEAVY MIDDLE!

Two years later, scientist Neils Bohr studied electrons. He suggested that electrons don't fly around randomly. He thought they traveled in a circle around the center of an atom.

Bohr thought that each electron needs a precise amount of energy to stay in its circle. When an electron gets more energy, it moves further away from the center.

NAILING THE NUCLEUS

Ernest Rutherford had a detailed plan to find out if atoms were empty. He shot particles at a thin piece of gold foil. If the atoms were empty, the particles would go through. Most did go through, but some bounced back. The particles were hitting the atom's solid nucleus.

CHAPTER 2

THE CURRENT ATOM MODEL

Today scientists know that an atom has three kinds of particles: electrons, protons, and neutrons. Out of the three particles, electrons are the only ones outside the nucleus.

Bohr was right that electrons move in different orbits depending on how much energy they have. But electrons don't travel in tight circles.

The electrons' paths are always changing. That's why scientists describe the area around the nucleus as an electron cloud.

HELLO???

Electrons have lots of room to travel. The electron cloud is about 10,000 times bigger than the width of the nucleus. If the nucleus was this ghost, some of the electrons would be more than 5 miles (8 kilometers) overhead.

TRRRRR

BOO!

An atom with a lot of electrons still has lots of empty space. An object like a tombstone looks and feels solid. But the atoms have a lot of empty space.

IMA GONER

But what about what's inside the nucleus? The protons and neutrons in a nucleus are too small to see. But they are enormous compared to electrons. If electrons were the size of fleas, protons and neutrons would be about as big as a large horse.

Atoms aren't all about size. They have mass too. To figure out the mass of an atom, you add the number of protons and the number of neutrons. This number is called the atomic mass. Electrons are so small that they aren't included in the atomic mass.

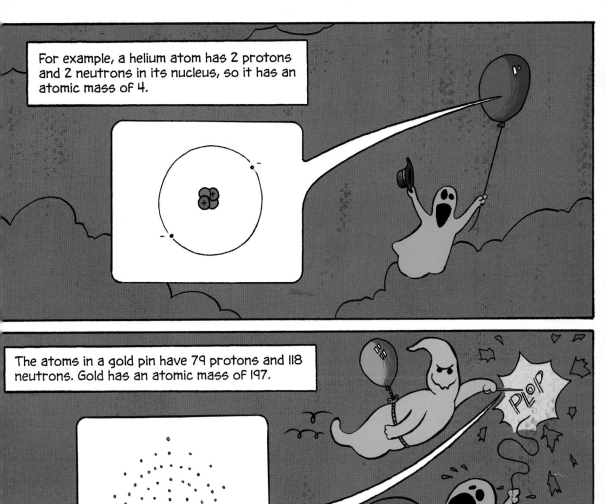

For example, a helium atom has 2 protons and 2 neutrons in its nucleus, so it has an atomic mass of 4.

The atoms in a gold pin have 79 protons and 118 neutrons. Gold has an atomic mass of 197.

QUARKY LITTLE THINGS

Electrons can't be divided any further. But scientists have found even smaller particles inside protons and neutrons. These particles are called quarks. Protons and neutrons each have three quarks. Some scientists believe there is nothing smaller inside a quark.

YOO-HOO!

Some of the particles in an atom are charged. Protons have a positive charge, and electrons have a negative charge. Neutrons don't have a charge.

Opposite charges attract each other, so electrons are attracted to protons. That's why electrons keep orbiting the nucleus instead of just flying away.

attract—to pull something closer

Particles with the same charge repel each other. Because electrons repel other electrons, they don't crash into each other as they orbit the nucleus.

PUNK!

CHUMP!

repel—to push something away

Each electron has one negative charge. Each proton has one positive charge. If you subtract the number of electrons from the number of protons, you get the atom's overall charge. Most atoms have the same number of protons and electrons, so their overall charge is zero.

THERE'S NO CHARGE FOR BEING NEUTRAL, DUDE.

Sometimes electrons get really fired up. They have so much energy that they break loose from their orbits around the nucleus. They leave their atoms and carry their negative charges with them.

YEE-HAW!

The atom that lost an electron is left with one more proton than electron. That means the atom is not neutral anymore. It has a positive charge. When an electron joins an atom, it gives the atom a negative charge. Atoms that are not neutral are called ions.

ARE YOU SURE YOU'RE AN ION?

YES, I'M POSITIVE!

SPEAK FOR YOURSELF ...

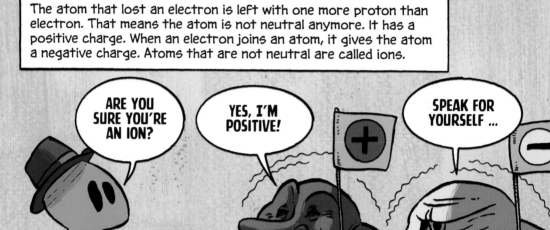

We get electricity from electrons that are on the move. People can control electricity by sending the electrons through metal wires.

The electrons power lights, radios, computers, and many other things. But watch out! Electricity can move through your body too.

Electrons in metals are only loosely connected to individual atoms, so they move easily. This makes metal a good conductor of electricity, which is why electrical wires are made of metal.

Plastic is not a good conductor, so electrical wires are wrapped in plastic. The plastic keeps you from getting a shock when you unplug your TV.

conductor—something that electricity moves through easily

ELECTRONS AND LIGHTNING

You can see electricity during a storm. Lightning occurs when lots of electrons move to another place very quickly. Electrons can move between clouds, as well as between the clouds and the ground.

OUCH!

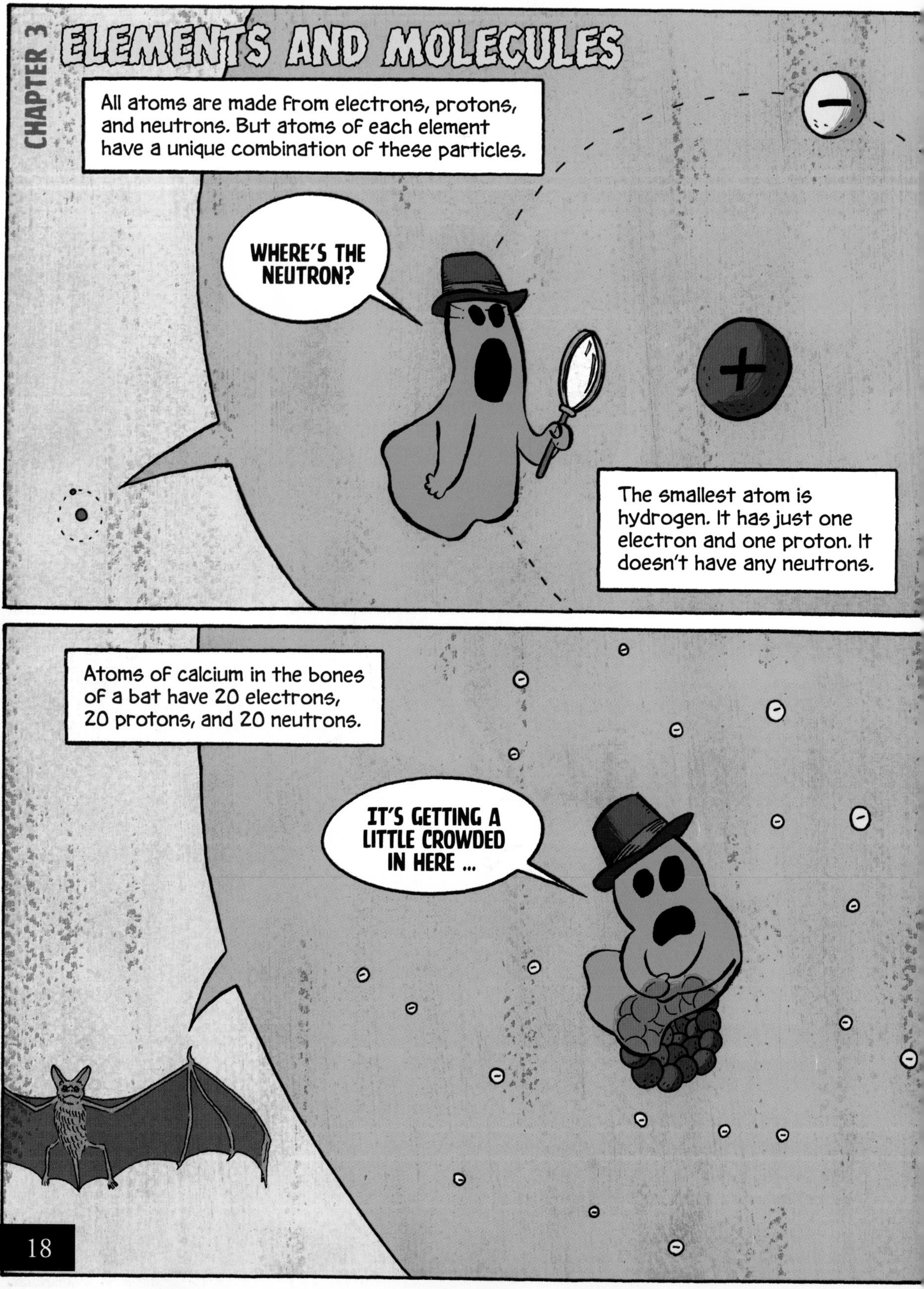
CHAPTER 3
ELEMENTS AND MOLECULES
All atoms are made from electrons, protons, and neutrons. But atoms of each element have a unique combination of these particles.
WHERE'S THE NEUTRON?
The smallest atom is hydrogen. It has just one electron and one proton. It doesn't have any neutrons.
Atoms of calcium in the bones of a bat have 20 electrons, 20 protons, and 20 neutrons.
IT'S GETTING A LITTLE CROWDED IN HERE ...

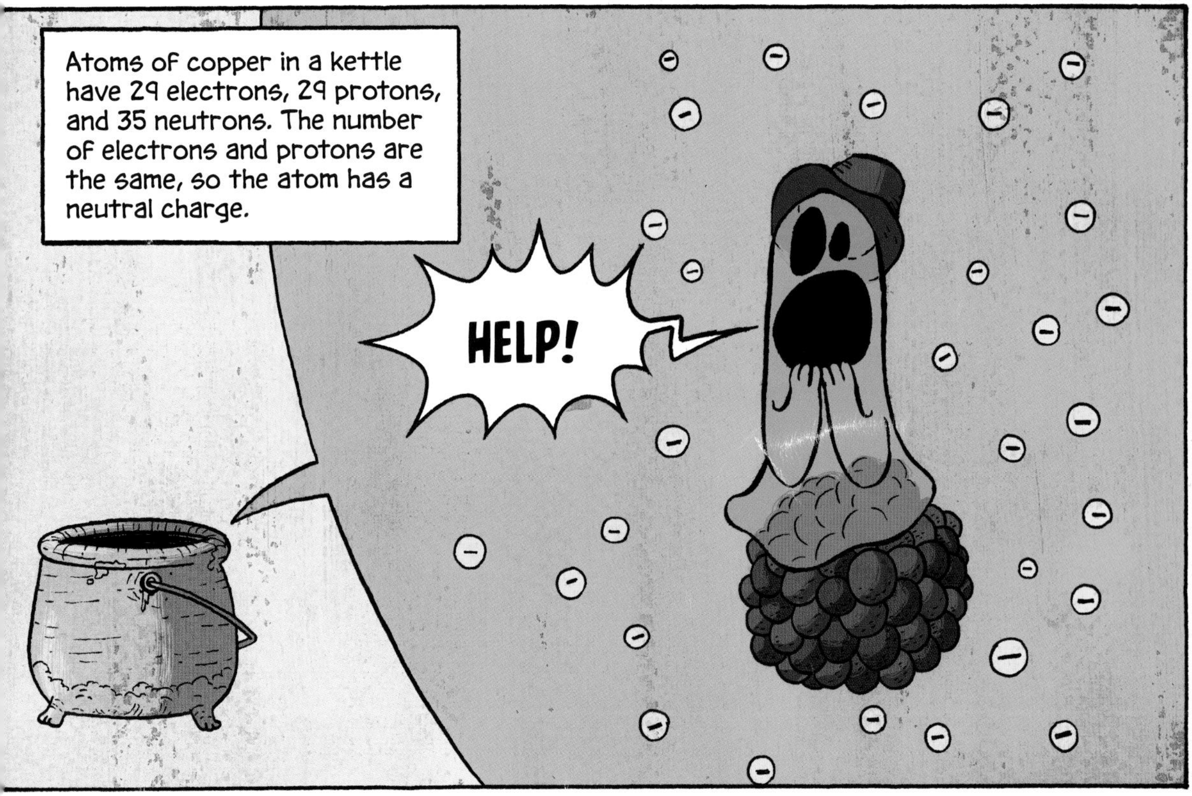
Atoms of copper in a kettle have 29 electrons, 29 protons, and 35 neutrons. The number of electrons and protons are the same, so the atom has a neutral charge.
HELP!

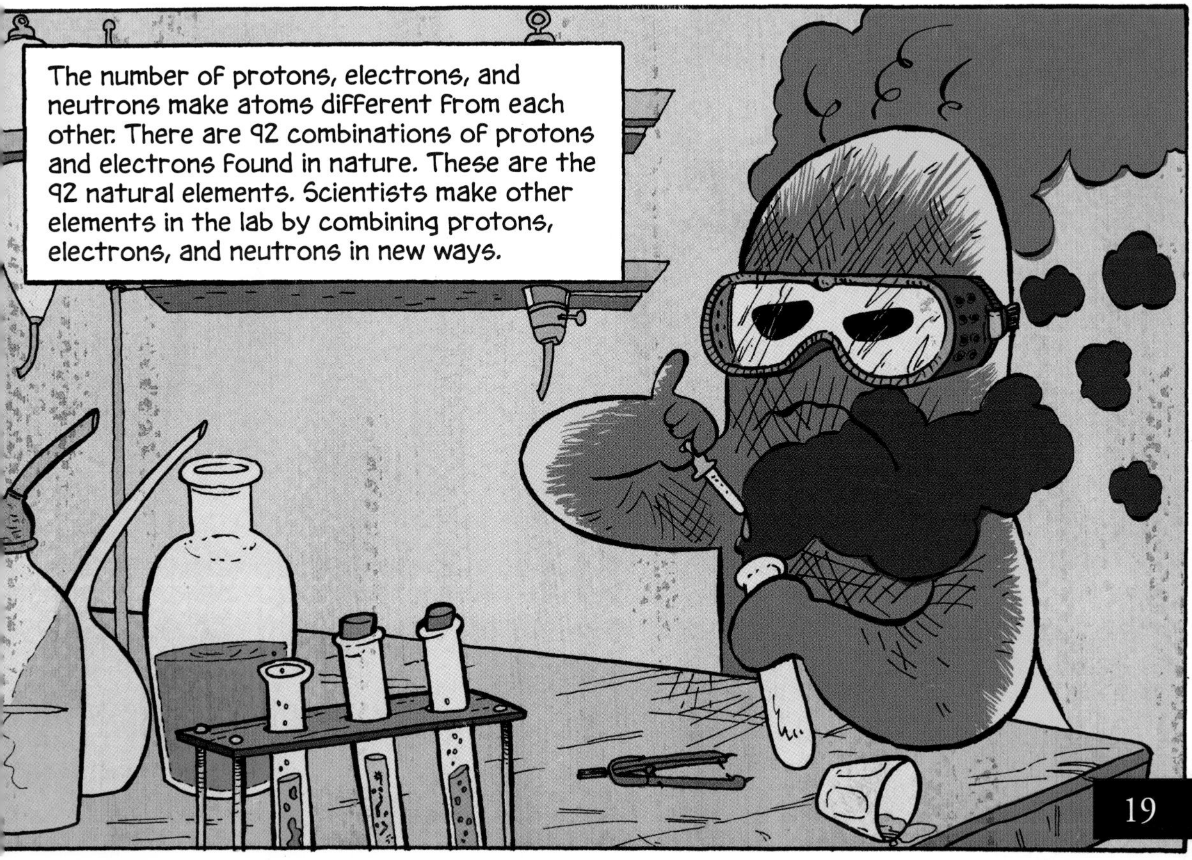
The number of protons, electrons, and neutrons make atoms different from each other. There are 92 combinations of protons and electrons found in nature. These are the 92 natural elements. Scientists make other elements in the lab by combining protons, electrons, and neutrons in new ways.

The number of protons and electrons is what defines an element. Take carbon, for example. Carbon atoms have six protons and six electrons.

YAAAHRR! A BEAUTIFUL DIAMOND. IT'S PURE CARBON.

If you took away a proton and an electron from a carbon atom, it wouldn't be carbon anymore. It would be boron.

WHAT DID YOU DO???

And if you added a proton and an electron to the carbon atom, it would become nitrogen, which is a gas.

ICE-O-WHAT?

On the other hand, atoms of the same element that have different numbers of neutrons are called isotopes.

For example, most carbon atoms have six neutrons. But some carbon atoms have seven or eight neutrons. So the atomic mass of carbon, which is 12, can actually be 13 or 14.

CARBON ISOTOPES

Scientists can use the isotopes of carbon to figure out how old an object is. Carbon-12 and carbon-13 atoms stay the same over time. But carbon-14 gradually breaks down into other atoms. Scientists look at how much carbon-14 is left to figure out how long a fossil, bone, or other ancient item has been around.

OLD. DEFINITELY OLD.

The world isn't made up of single elements. Most things have more than one element. For example, the smallest part of water is a group of three atoms: one oxygen atom and two hydrogen atoms. Groups of atoms that stick together are called molecules.

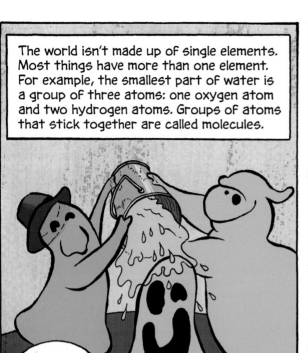

METHANE

Molecules are described by the elements they have in them. You've probably heard water called H_2O. That's because it has two hydrogen atoms (H) and one oxygen atom (O). Methane gas is written as CH_4 because it has one carbon atom and four hydrogen atoms.

Molecules act differently than their elements do alone. For example, water is a liquid at room temperature. But oxygen and hydrogen alone are both gases!

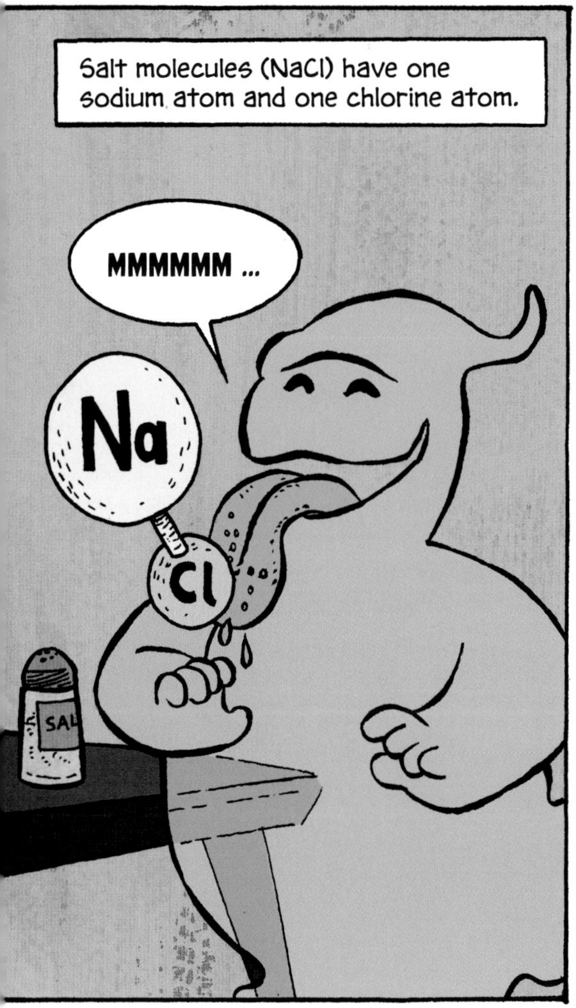
Salt molecules (NaCl) have one sodium atom and one chlorine atom.
MMMMMM ...
Na
Cl
SAL

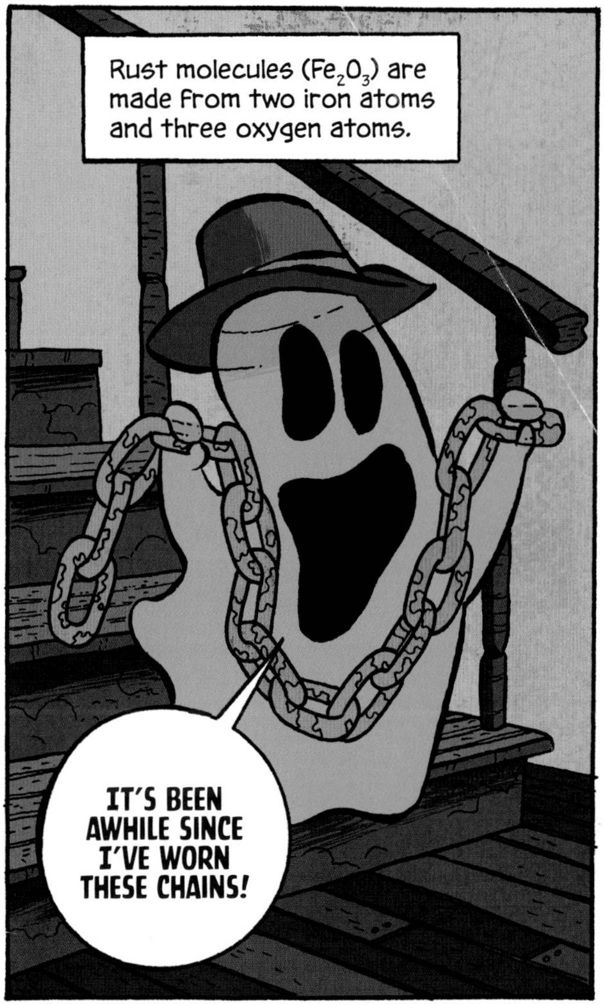
Rust molecules (Fe_2O_3) are made from two iron atoms and three oxygen atoms.
IT'S BEEN AWHILE SINCE I'VE WORN THESE CHAINS!

MOLECULAR CHAINS

Rubber molecules are huge. They can have billions of atoms of carbon and hydrogen joined together. These molecules are made of combinations of smaller molecules. The smaller molecules are joined together in a chain.

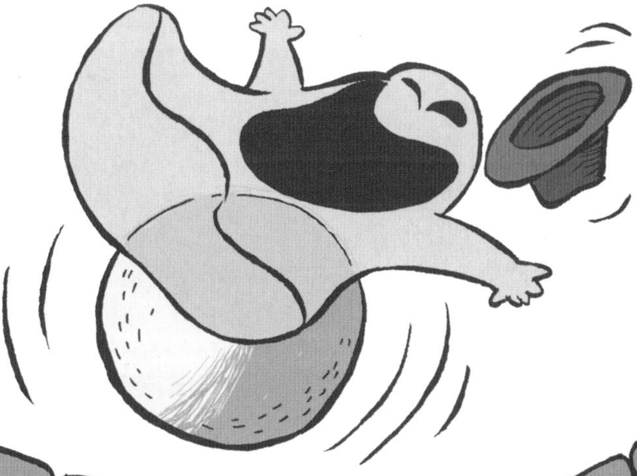

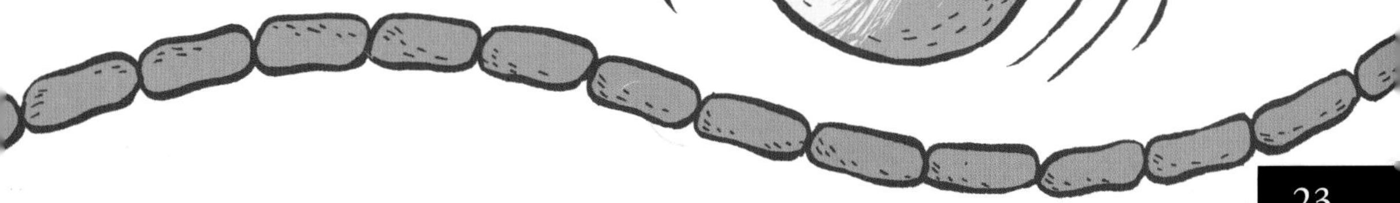

We know that water is always made up of two hydrogen atoms and one oxygen atom. So how can water be a solid, a liquid, and a gas?

AM I A SOLID, A LIQUID, OR A GAS?

Atoms and molecules are always jiggling around, even in an object that looks like it's not moving. How fast molecules move depends on how much heat is present. If there's more heat, the molecules move faster.

YEP, HE'S MOVING PRETTY FAST!

In most of the things around us, atoms and molecules move slowly and stay close together. These objects are called solids. When water has little heat, it becomes ice.

When atoms and molecules become hotter, they move faster. At faster speeds, they don't stay together as well. Then the object becomes a liquid.

If atoms and molecules are heated a lot, they move extremely fast. The molecules are no longer close together, and the material becomes a gas.

Gases, liquids, and solids are all states of matter.

CHAPTER 4

STUDYING ATOMS AND MOLECULES

Because atoms and molecules are so tiny, scientists use models to show what they look like. Using models, we can learn a lot about the makeup and structure of atoms and molecules.

COULD YOU TURN A LITTLE TO THE LEFT?

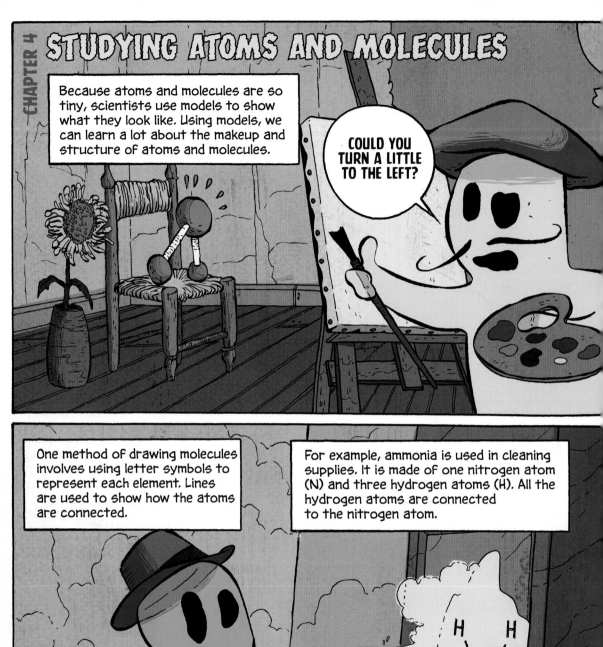

One method of drawing molecules involves using letter symbols to represent each element. Lines are used to show how the atoms are connected.

For example, ammonia is used in cleaning supplies. It is made of one nitrogen atom (N) and three hydrogen atoms (H). All the hydrogen atoms are connected to the nitrogen atom.

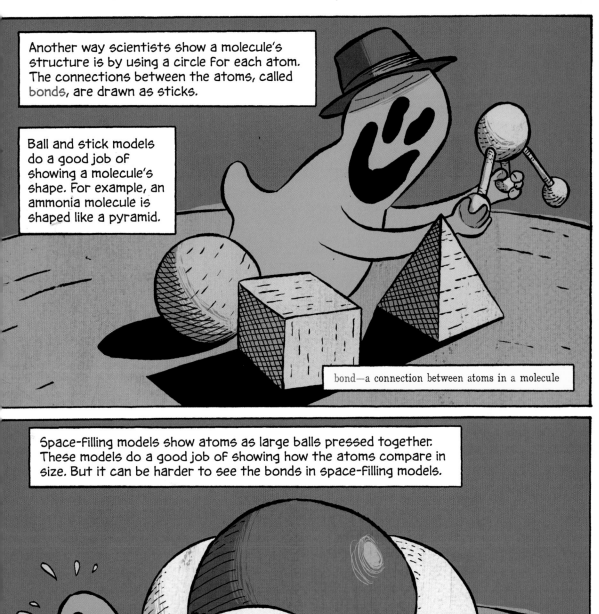

Another way scientists show a molecule's structure is by using a circle for each atom. The connections between the atoms, called bonds, are drawn as sticks.

Ball and stick models do a good job of showing a molecule's shape. For example, an ammonia molecule is shaped like a pyramid.

bond—a connection between atoms in a molecule

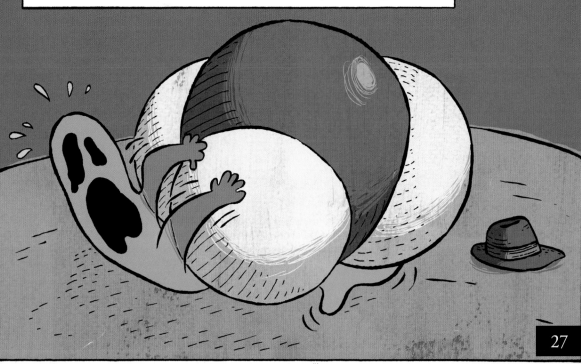

Space-filling models show atoms as large balls pressed together. These models do a good job of showing how the atoms compare in size. But it can be harder to see the bonds in space-filling models.

Although we know a lot about atoms, scientists are always discovering new things about them. Complex equipment helps scientists with their research on atoms.

Particle Accelerator

Much of this research takes place inside particle accelerators. These huge machines help scientists look for particles. The machines work by crashing particles into each other at very high speeds.

LOOK OUT!

Scientists study the results of the crash to see if the particles are destroyed and if new particles are created.

Scientists use machines to detect the outline of atoms. A pointer with an atom-sized tip rubs across the surface of a material. The tip bumps up and down as it hits atoms. A computer uses information about the bumps to create a picture of the atoms.

Scientists have also found ways to use atoms. There is a lot of energy stored inside an atom's nucleus. Energy is released when the nucleus breaks apart. Nuclear power plants smash neutrons into atoms to release the energy inside. The energy is used to generate electricity.

Today's scientists continue to learn more about the tiny atoms that make up our world. Who knows what we'll discover next about these tiny building blocks of matter!

I'LL BET WE'RE MADE OF ATOMS TOO ...

GLOSSARY

atom (AT-uhm)—a tiny particle that is a basic building block of matter

attract (uh-TRAKT)—to pull something closer

bond (BOHND)—a connection between atoms in a molecule

conductor (kuhn-DUHK-tur)—something that electricity moves through easily

electron (i-LEK-tron)—a negatively charged particle found inside an atom

element (EL-uh-muhnt)—a substance consisting of a single type of atom

isotope (EYE-soh-tope)—atoms that have the same number of protons but different numbers of neutrons in the nucleus

mass (MASS)—a measure of the number and density of the atoms in an object

matter (MAT-ur)—anything that has mass and takes up space

molecule (MOL-uh-kyool)—a group of connected atoms

neutron (NOO-tron)—an uncharged particle found in the nucleus of an atom

nucleus (NOO-klee-uhss)—the heavy, dense center of an atom

particle (PAR-tuh-kuhl)—a very small piece or amount of something

proton (PROH-ton)—a positively charged particle found in the nucleus of an atom

quark (KWORK)—an atomic particle that is smaller than a neutron or proton

repel (ri-PEL)—to push something away

READ MORE

Aloian, Molly. *Atoms and Molecules.* Why Chemistry Matters. New York: Crabtree Pub. Co., 2009.

Slade, Suzanne. *The Structure of Atoms.* The Library of Physical Science. New York: Rosen Pub. Group's PowerKids Press, 2007.

Spilsbury, Louise, and Richard Spilsbury. *Atoms and Molecules.* Building Blocks of Matter. Chicago, Ill.: Heinemann Library, 2007.

INTERNET SITES

FactHound offers a safe, fun way to find Internet sites related to this book. All sites on FactHound have been researched by our staff.

Here's all you do:

Visit www.facthound.com

Type in this code: 9781429665810

Check out projects, games and lots more at
www.capstonekids.com

Super-cool stuff!

INDEX